GET QUOTIVATED!

166 Quotable Insights to Catapult Creativity

by

Jimmy Leo

Copyright © 2013 Jimmy Leo
All rights reserved.
ISBN: 0615751385
ISBN 13: 9780615751382

Dedicated to my mother, Eileen Leo, and the memory of my father, Michael Leo. Thank you both for being my first teachers in life.

"Jimmy Leo presents life lessons and management enhancement in a fun filled, fresh and entertaining atmosphere. Jimmy's artistry, creativity, and skills are original and thought provoking, and are used in a progressive fashion. Highly interactive, his style prompts participants to think in alternate ways and to understand the solutions to their problems by seeing them in a new light."

–Carson Schaffer, President
–Terra Cloud, Inc.

"Jimmy Leo delivers a most unique message: Humor with a velvet punch. He invites all participants into the deeper questions of life, like why am I here and what am I supposed to do next? Jimmy's performances are life changing and motivational"

–Ken Donaldson, LMHC
–Author of "Marry Yourself First"

"His messages really resonated. They were really LISTENING to what he was saying....even though he was so entertaining with his performance, they heard his story too. The format of his talk was CAPTIVATING! The audience was truly wrapped in how he was demonstrating his artistry and it's constant connection to the audience."

–Georgianna Valle, Author/Advocate
–National Alliance on Mental Illness

"I saw Jimmy Leo give a talk early in 2012 that was hilarious and poignant at the same time. He captured the audience's attention and elicited many emotions as he gave suggestions to people on managing their lives."

–Jim Delvecchio, author, speaker
–"Manifesting Abundance: The Universal Key"

"Jimmy is an outstanding educational presenter! This man knows how to involve audiences in very creative ways. His wit and wisdom . . . plus a delightful dash of humor . . . are signatures of his energetic presentations. Jimmy also shines as an author, where his book shares an important message. I've personally learned from Jimmy's approach, improving what I do in my own speaking presentations. Thanks for showing me new ways to communicate."

Kathleen Rehl – Speaker, Author of "Moving Forward on your Own"

ACKNOWLEDGEMENTS

First and foremost, I would like to thank God for the gifts and opportunities He has given me, and for the responsibility to share them with those around me.

I would like to thank my mother and father for their nonstop support through all these years in my numerous endeavors. I appreciate the model they have set for me as parents and people in general. Finally, I am eternally grateful for their never-ending, unconditional love. Parenting didn't come with a handbook, but they did an amazing job just the same.

My wife, Donna, and my daughters, Miranda and Emily, have been my rocks through this entire process. I can never thank them enough for all they have given me. They are my life, and everything I have would mean nothing if I didn't have them to share it with. Also, I would get a severe tongue lashing if I didn't mention that my family also includes Princess (our dog), Pumpkin (the hamster), and Bluey and Bluebell (our fish). As my daughters often remind me, our pets are an important part of our family.

A special thanks to my wife, Donna, for looking me in the eye one day and telling me to chase my dream at any cost. For a while, I forgot the importance of effectively chasing a dream. Donna made it clear that I should take whatever chances needed to be taken, break whatever rules needed to be broken, listen to my heart only, and forget the necessary costs along the way. She has become my hero, and I love her so very much.

Special thanks to my mentor and friend, Delatorro McNeal II. A person can have all of the tools, gifts, and abilities in the world, but coupled with the wrong mind-set will go nowhere. Delatorro is the man who changed my mind, and in effect changed my ability to benefit others. He is the model of what an ideal mentor should be. He's the one who showed me my potential and helped me realize how many people out there can benefit from my teachings. Thank you, Del.

To my accountability partners and friends, Terri Bork, Jenny Olding, and Stanley and Edwich Poitevien: thanks for keeping me in line, and thanks for hearing every idea I threw at you. I appreciate you all very much.

I must give a special thank you to Kathy Potts for steering me in the direction of Delatorro. Also, thanks for being such a great friend and spending so much time listening…and helping to get me unstuck.

To David Glickman, I appreciate you for helping me see that I was due for a metamorphosis from performer to professional speaker. Sometimes objects are closer than they appear, and we need the help of someone near us to point them out. Thanks for taking the time to point it out, David.

I am forever grateful to the members of the Quantum Coaching Program and the "Live Your Speaking Dreams" class of 2012. I will always appreciate Rosilyn Dickerson, Elaine Hocker, Karim Ellis, Anthony Fisher, Noelle Kelman, and Stanley Poitevien. You have helped me become what I am meant to be. Thank you for that wondrous feat.

I am also grateful to the central Florida chapter of NSA (National Speakers Association). I have received tremendous content, skills, and feedback from so many wonderful members of what is clearly one of the greatest groups of minds to assemble.

Finally, I would like to point out what a huge influence my brother has been to me. Though I have never really told him, I have always looked up to him and spent many years trying to be more like him. I'm lucky to have Mike Leo in my life.

PREFACE

"Without cartoons, life is just a MESS!" – Anonymous

List five cartoons you enjoy watching when you need to unwind. If you don't watch any, try watching some.

When a student in one of my classes first told me this, he said it with certain levity. As time wore on that day, I thought about the statement and, because of the great truth within it, found it quotable. In finding it quotable, I began thinking about it on a regular basis. It would lead me to ask a consistent series of questions. With a bit of time, the quote itself went by the wayside, but the habit of consistent questioning stayed in me. This resulted in some incredible discoveries as I took a journey to better understand myself, my gifts, my impact on others, and my place in this world.

Like many others, I have spent years searching the world for the answers to my many questions. My life has proven to be an interesting one: from my days working as a bellhop in a leading hotel chain, to my days running my own business entertaining others, to my days as an educator. I started to understand my gifts, but failed to find answers to the other, more important, questions within me.

The more I questioned others, the more varied the answers I received. I no longer knew which answers were right, or, for that matter, if they could possibly *all* be correct…or only correct specifically to those people. As it turns out, the latter was the case, which still left me wondering: Who *was* I meant to benefit in this world? What was my purpose? Who was I? What was my place in the grand scheme of things?

Have you been there? Have you wondered these same thoughts? Have other questions plagued you as well? Has seeking the answers left you feeling even more lost than when you started? Have you ever felt as if life should offer you more? When was the last time you felt *completely* in charge of your destiny? If any of these questions resonate with you, know that you are not alone. Millions feel the way you do, but seldom discuss it for fear that others may not be able to relate. Let's face it: the big questions are, for lack of a better term, big! That's why many people fail to even ask them. Of the ones who do, many have a fear of being ostracized, and though they may start the process of seeking answers, they rarely stay the course.

The ones who keep asking eventually discover something incredible. The answers aren't out in the world, but rather within themselves. A certain renewed energy takes over with the realization that the answers, like the questions, are tucked deep inside. All it takes is an internal search rather than an external quest. Once that realization sweeps over you, you will notice more questions emerge with those answers inside you. Suddenly you will discover that, far from being the giant question mark you have always imagined, you are actually a huge book filled with an incredible amount of information, and you've barely skimmed the table of contents. The more you start learning about yourself, the more you will *want* to learn.

As I continued discovering answers internally, I realized that I may not be alone, that others out there likely struggled with some of these same questions. A large part of the process became scaling the internal mountain to gain more knowledge of myself while also reaching back to those who shared the place I used to occupy and still struggled with their identities and purposes in life. In reaching backward to benefit them, a greater connection developed on the external level. The tapestry of communication and socialization developed at its highest level.

My ability to benefit others proved a gift when I worked as a bellhop. As an entertainer, I found a gift in developing a connection with others: in helping them escape their daily lives, in making them laugh, and in keeping them both amazed and entertained. Through entertaining, I discovered my other calling: educating. Though the instruction started informally during my presentations, it soon took on a formal nature when I became a professional educator. I had also realized that I can weave these gifts and talents together in a manner that serves others. Ultimately, I could use my creative expertise to develop something unique that benefits many people all at once. With that, I started work on what you are holding right now. This is our connection.

I took a great deal of what I had already learned and put it in the form of quotations. When complete, I sent it to my mentor, Delatorro McNeal. "Jim, that quote book is a beast," he smiled enthusiastically. "Now you have to put in some action steps."

I felt good…for three fleeting seconds. "Action steps?" I asked.

"Jim, quotes are great, but you need a way for readers to take the quotes and apply them directly into their lives."

Delatorro was right and I knew it. When I lectured on performance at entertainment conventions, I would frequently teach other entertainers about the importance of blurring the line between the performer and the audience. I would lecture on the importance of the audience *being* the show, not just seeing the show. Delatorro was correct: I shouldn't just write a book others would read; I should create something readers would use and reuse constantly. After all, we are constantly changing, and therefore need to reconnect with ourselves on a regular basis.

Do *not* think of this as just another book; it offers far more than any book could. It is a tool designed to help you gain a greater understanding of yourself, where your talents and gifts rest, who might benefit from them, and how the world will benefit from your being in it. Do not think of the action steps as chores by any means, but rather as interesting ways to get better acquainted with the most fascinating person in the world: *You*. Finally, consider the quotes little pieces of information to jumpstart your brain into thinking more deeply on a regular basis. When the creative mind kicks in—and it will—you will be amazed at the capabilities you discover within yourself.

You will also notice that the end of this book offers up a series of tools used throughout the book itself: Venn diagrams, journal entries, rating lists, and more. These tools serve teachers well in classrooms around the world and will serve their purpose here as well. Take the time to look deeper into these tools and take them beyond these pages. Learn to use them in your everyday life and see how much more organized you become, as well as how much more attuned you become to yourself and those around you.

It sounds like a lot of thinking and doing and preparing, doesn't it? Perception is key. Tap into your creativity and see this as a fun journey rather than a distant destination. Honestly, if taken in all at once, it may seem a bit overwhelming. If it does, just refer back to that very first quote and the action step that goes with it. As a wise man once said, "Life without cartoons is just a mess!" Good luck with your journey, fellow traveler.

1

> The changes we don't make for fear of the unknowns that wait on the other side are often the changes that can be made at the hands of others anyway.

ACTION STEP

List five times in your life when change happened to you at the hands of someone else (a new school, a new home, a new job, a recent move). Explain how things could have more positively benefited you had *you* made the changes for yourself instead.

1) _____

2) _____

3) _____

4) _____

5) _____

2

> *If, out of fear, you refuse to change, life's constant forward movement ensures change will happen anyway.*

ACTION STEP

List three areas of your life that are deeply impacted by your inability to change. For each area mentioned, state at least one different course your life could take instead if you embraced the change you fear so much.

1) _____

2) _____

3) _____

3

> That tiny voice in your head tells you negative things for a reason. Having no physical body, it has never been able to do anything to feel the power of achievement.

ACTION STEP

Write ten achievements you have accomplished and think back to what made them so special. What made you ignore that negative voice at those times?

1) _____

2) _____

3) _____

4) _____

5) _____

6) _____

7) _____

8) _____

9) _____

10) _____

4

If that voice has never experienced success, how can it be expected to encourage you? Ignore your negative "in your head" voice.

ACTION STEP

Think back to a time when you gave advice on a subject with which you had no personal experience. How was your advice received? Was the other person's reaction justified? What steps can you take to ensure your advice may be better heeded next time?

1) _____

2) _____

3) _____

4) _____

5) _____

5

It's amazing that we give credence to the negative words in our heads, but when asked to give them a face, a name, a personality, etc., we can't seem to do it.

ACTION STEP

Close your eyes and visualize the appearance that goes with the negative voice in your head. While you're at it, practice making that appearance smaller and less valuable so as to give it little or no worth.

1) _____

2) _____

3) _____

4) _____

5) _____

6

Knowledge is $ellable.

ACTION STEP

Draw a Venn diagram in which the left circle represents your areas of education and the right circle represents your areas of experience. The middle area should represent things that demonstrate financial value in any way, shape, or form. These items could include financial assets, property, real estate, income, inheritance, investments, etc. The middle section *may* be larger than the two outer portions put together, and you should have a visual of just how financially valuable you really are. Are you content with what this reveals about your current financial value? If not, what can be done to change it? Where can you go to gain information on how to increase your financial value?

1) _____

2) _____

3) _____

4) _____

5) _____

7

> Knowledge holds value that can be paid either in effort, time, or money.

ACTION STEP

Given that we normally think in terms of knowledge giving us financial value, name five ways in which knowledge can give you value in terms of time, and five ways in terms of effort. For example, cooking in a microwave instead of a regular oven gives additional time that could be spent with family or friends. Delegating smaller work tasks can allow us additional energy for other tasks requiring greater focus or effort.

1) _____

2) _____

3) _____

4) _____

5) _____

8

The more that senses come into play, the greater the chances of learning.

ACTION STEP

Take a moment and think back to some of your previous years in school. What years held the greatest learning for you? Why? What types of learning (auditory, visual, tactile, etc., or a combination thereof) did you most enjoy and why?

1) _____

2) _____

3) _____

4) _____

5) _____

9

If you're unable to give 100 percent toward making yourself happy, you'll never be able to give 100 percent toward making others happy.

ACTION STEP

Think of a situation in which you focused on gaining happiness through first giving it to someone else. Did that happiness feel fulfilling? Did it feel slightly hollow? If you felt fulfilled, can you elaborate on how it was achieved? If it felt hollow, what could be done instead to achieve fulfillment?

1) _____

2) _____

3) _____

4) _____

5) _____

10

Investment—It's not whether you can afford to go, it's whether you can afford not to go.

ACTION STEP

Give careful thought to opportunities in your life that called for investments you chose not to make. Write down three, and explore how the path of your life would have changed as a result. Now think of three present opportunities and three potential opportunities for the future. How might you approach those opportunities to your greatest benefit?

1) _____

2) _____

3) _____

11

> Someone's "useless" is another person's gold.

ACTION STEP

Given that this applies to tangible things, list ten things you might consider useless that someone else may consider gold. How could you invest your time and effort to get this gold into someone else's hands? What kind of impact might it have on someone else's life?

1) _____

2) _____

3) _____

4) _____

5) _____

6) _____

7) _____

8) _____

9) _____

10) _____

12

> If people won't listen to it, there's no sense in saying it, no matter how important it seems.

ACTION STEP

Identify three times in your life when you tried to communicate something important but the recipients refused to intently listen. What were the results of these situations? Determine how you might have altered your delivery to help others better grasp your point.

1) _____

2) _____

3) _____

13

> *Children get it:
> Knowledge starts
> with good questions.*

ACTION STEP

Outline a series of at least ten questions—start with broad questions on an already known topic for the purpose of understanding the process. Eventually, narrow the series to questions you may not know the answers to and do further research. How does this method of questioning tie in to your best methods of learning? Some of the best methods of learning include auditory (listening), tactile (touching or manipulating things), visual (such as graphs, charts, and highlights), and experiential (experiencing a lesson firsthand)

1) _____

2) _____

3) _____

4) _____

5) _____

14

> *Challenges stimulate personal growth. Appreciate them as such.*

ACTION STEP

Using a Frayer diagram (please see diagram section in the rear of book) with the word "Challenges" in the center, document five challenges you have faced (upper left quadrant); the negative aspects they possessed (upper right quadrant); the benefits of those challenges (lower left quadrant); and the changes that occurred in your life as a result (lower right quadrant). How would you interpret the data from this diagram? What can be learned from it? How can you benefit from the future as a result of better understanding this new look at challenges?

1) _____

2) _____

3) _____

4) _____

5) _____

15

> *Taking action, no matter how small, is still better than continued contemplation.*

ACTION STEP

Name seven milestones in your life that required action to be taken. On a separate piece of paper, indicate the direction your life may have taken had no action been associated with those milestones.

1) _____

2) _____

3) _____

4) _____

5) _____

6) _____

7) _____

16

> "I love lasagna; it's filled with a variety of foods I love, all put together. Finding your passion or purpose is like finding lasagna."

ACTION STEP

For ten focused, uninterrupted minutes, list as many of your likes as you possibly can. When you have finished, try categorizing them in groups. Considering the different aspects of life (spiritual, professional, personal, relational, mental, physical), how can you combine your many likes into something purposeful, or something you are passionate about? How could it benefit others?

1) _____

2) _____

3) _____

4) _____

5) _____

17

> Currency is not a dollar amount; it's anything you have of value to both you and others that can be exchanged for other needs or wants.

ACTION STEP

From baseball cards to bottle caps to bracelets, name an assortment of currency you have possessed in your life that was not dollar-related. Can you now explain how much wealth is correlated to money? Using percent, can you state how much of your wealth you attributed to money before today? Do you attribute the same amount now? Why or why not? What other forms of wealth occupy your life that you hadn't considered as wealth before? How does this impact you knowing they are now being seen as a form of wealth?

1) _____

2) _____

3) _____

4) _____

5) _____

18

> Wealth is value, simply stated. Be it family, friends, money, time, effort, convenience, tangible luxuries, etc., wealth is anything that holds value to you.

ACTION STEP

Name eight different forms of wealth. What roles do these forms of wealth play in your life and why?

1) _____

2) _____

3) _____

4) _____

5) _____

6) _____

7) _____

8) _____

19

> *The correct question shouldn't be "How do I make more money?" but rather "How can I leverage my wealth to further benefit those around me, thus prompting reciprocity?"*

ACTION STEP

Create a story about yourself. Be sure each point of interest in the story demonstrates some wealth you gained from someone else as a result of doing something for them first. For instance, as a result of babysitting for a little girl at a critical moment, her parents name their newborn child after you. Be sure to list responsibilities that came with the new role. Point out any conflicts, events, or resolutions along the way. Using a story map, illustrate the story of your life and the wealth you have obtained as a result of reciprocity. Be sure to include characters, settings, conflict, events, and resolutions.. In my own situation, I started entertaining adults and children, with comedy & balloon artistry, making children and adults feel special. In return, I have been rewarded with money, favors, & smiles from children & parents alike. What wealth did you receive as a result of reciprocity from something you first offered?

1) _____

2) _____

3) _____

4) _____

5) _____

20

A positively directed attitude is the precursor to gaining wealth

ACTION STEP

Using a cause-and-effect chart, list three situations that involved a change in your attitude toward work, home, or faith. In each case, list the causes and effects as well as the event. What correlation do you see between the causes and the effects? What correlation is noticed between the causes or effects and the particular event that they deal with?

1) _____

2) _____

3) _____

4) _____

5) _____

21

There are two directions of attitude: internal and external. Only a lucky few realize that to truly reap external wealth, they must fully sow their internal direction.

ACTION STEP

Using the same chart from the previous quote, list three examples of internal direction of attitude and three examples of external direction of attitude. Include their causes and their effects. Understand that internal direction of attitude is focusing inward in regard to resolving needs & desires and external direction of attitude is a focus outward benefiting the needs & desires of others. For instance, quitting a job that you know wasn't providing you with what you needed may have resulted in a sense of empowerment that encouraged you to share empowerment with those around you.

1) _____

2) _____

3) _____

22

The difference between reciprocation and obligation is a desire to assist in return.

ACTION STEP

Create a list of professional & personal situations in which people may have felt obligated to assist you. Do the same in the second column for situations in which you feel people reciprocated out of desire to repay your kindness. What differences may have existed in the attitudes of those people toward you in the two situations?

1) _____

2) _____

3) _____

4) _____

5) _____

23

The difference between getting what you need and getting what you want is the difference between a scowl and a smile.

ACTION STEP

Define attitude as it applies to you. Briefly write how your attitude has affected others around you, both negatively and positively.

1) _____

2) _____

3) _____

4) _____

5) _____

24

*The best way to understand internal versus external direction of attitude is to carefully examine a laugh.
It happens entirely because of something you process in your mind that makes you happy in some way, but the laugh itself is shared externally with others surrounding you, contagiously spreading a positive attitude like a wildfire.*

ACTION STEP

Take a moment and think of anything you find humorous. Think about the reaction of those around you when you laugh out loud. Knowing the positive impact laughter causes, actively try to make people around you laugh three times daily.

1) _____

2) _____

3) _____

4) _____

5) _____

25

> Other people's opinions are only as powerful as you allow them to be.

ACTION STEP

For one week, take people's opinions to heart and journal how it makes you feel. Then spend a week focusing on allowing your own opinion to be the one that is most powerful and journal your feelings again. Do you feel differently when you give power to others rather than take hold of it yourself?

1) _____

2) _____

3) _____

4) _____

5) _____

26

Opinions appear like shadows; they seem huge and loom over us, when in reality they cannot be touched and will disappear with the emergence of light.

ACTION STEP

Browse the history of your life and list seven people who intimidated you in some way. When you stood up for yourself, what kind of reaction did you receive? Did the other person back down? Did he or she seem as intimidating afterwards, or perhaps more human?

1) _____

2) _____

3) _____

4) _____

5) _____

27

Happiness in what you do stems from happiness in who you are.

ACTION STEP

List ten positive qualities about yourself. How does your focus on these positive qualities impact the reactions of those around you? If necessary, take a week and log your qualities in situations and the results from those around you.

1) _____

2) _____

3) _____

4) _____

5) _____

6) _____

7) _____

8) _____

9) _____

10) _____

28

Opening yourself up to the unknown makes you more willing to understand it.

ACTION STEP

Name three occasions as a child when you experienced something new. How did you respond to the experience? Name three similar recent occasions. Are you more or less willing to open up to the unknown now? Why?

1) _____

2) _____

3) _____

29

> Obligation drives people to act because they feel they have to; it is giving at its bare minimum, without desire. Reciprocation prompts people to act because they genuinely want to. It is giving at its maximum, done out of appreciation over a previously shared value from another person.

ACTION STEP

Given one specific example in your life (professional, personal, etc.), compare the results you get from people who give based on a feeling of obligation as opposed to those who give out of genuine desire. Which people give more? What insight might they gain? from one column over the other?

1) _____

2) _____

3) _____

4) _____

5) _____

30

Serving others creates a positive ripple effect. Like a single stone tossed into the water, service allows for positive, exponential growth and change in all directions.

ACTION STEP

Draw a series of concentric circles representing the pond with the ripples. In the center circle, write down a purposeful event in your life. In the outer circles, list the various levels of people who benefited from that event, with whom they may have shared that benefit, and how. For example, a person in an accident might have her life saved by a doctor, positively impacting her as well as her family and friends. She may study to be a doctor to save lives as hers was saved. In return hundreds of lives are saved by her and thousands of friends and family are grateful for it.

1) _____

2) _____

3) _____

4) _____

5) _____

31

If in five seconds your one smile positively impacted five people who then passed it on with the same result, your exponential smile will have positively impacted 244,140,625 people in only a minute. Smiles go far!

ACTION STEP

Today, as you go through your day, smile and pleasantly greet as many people as you can. Count the number of smiles or pleasantries returned to you.

1) _____

2) _____

3) _____

4) _____

5) _____

32

No matter how much effort you put into it, the workload never seems to diminish. Workload change comes not from the amount of time put into the tasks, but rather in adjusting the mind-set toward the work. Do the work systematically. You will accomplish it with less effort and in an equal amount of time.

ACTION STEP

Create a task list and focus only on what's on the list. Should new tasks arise throughout the day, you may add them in, but limit yourself to five new tasks. Focus more on accomplishing what's already on the list.

1) _____

2) _____

3) _____

4) _____

5) _____

33

The next time you think you're amazing, take a look up. Blue skies, billowy white clouds, amazing sunrises and sunsets, and constellations lining the night sky. Allow yourself to be humbled, understanding your place in the grand scheme of things.

ACTION STEP

As you go through your day, slow your pace and look in directions you normally don't look. Take notice of the beauty and wonder that surround you every day, both natural and man-made.

1) _____

2) _____

3) _____

4) _____

5) _____

34

> Not being as important as you think you are means not having to shoulder as much as you think you do.

ACTION STEP

Name five people in your life who can help take some of the load off of your shoulders or provide you with a better perspective on handling your life.

1) _____

2) _____

3) _____

4) _____

5) _____

35

> Take a deep breath, hold it, and exhale. It's never as bad as it seems.

ACTION STEP

Each morning for five minutes, close your eyes and breathe. Focus on breathing consistently and slowly. Carefully adjust the speed of your breathing to become slower and slower. Let your mind focus only on your breathing and the relaxed state it brings. Take careful note of any thoughts or ideas that suddenly pop into your head. . Should you try to suppress them? If so, how? If these thoughts prove negative, can you try to focus on their opposite? If they prove positive, how can you maintain consistency?

1) _____

2) _____

3) _____

4) _____

5) _____

36

When in doubt, look at an adverse situation in a manner you never have before. It offers beneficial truths and lessons.

ACTION STEP

Take a few minutes to visualize yourself as a person who welcomes adversity and champions tough times for the lessons and wisdom they provide. See yourself encountering a full day of obstacles, and turning them into benefits for yourself or others. Write down everything you visualized. Who did it benefit and how?

1) _____

2) _____

3) _____

4) _____

5) _____

37

When you have too much on your mind, look to the stars for support.

ACTION STEP

Look to something far grander than yourself to put yourself and your thoughts in perspective. It can be the night sky, the billowy clouds, or lightning in a thunderstorm. Allow these wonders to shrink the size of the things on your mind.

1) _____

2) _____

3) _____

4) _____

5) _____

38

If you're busy ensuring you're just like everyone else, all you'll successfully do is blend in to a point of anonymity. If being unnoticed by a single soul is your goal… mission accomplished.

ACTION STEP

What have you purposely done today that caused you to stand out in some positive way? In the past week? The past month? The past year?

1) _____

2) _____

3) _____

4) _____

5) _____

39

The more people say something can't be done, the greater the likelihood that it can.

ACTION STEP

Write a brief diary entry about a time when you wanted to do something but felt discouraged by others. Explain what you think their reasoning may be. How did you respond? Did you still try despite efforts to dissuade you?. Describe your feelings and emotions in depth and how they tied into your efforts.

1) _____

2) _____

3) _____

4) _____

5) _____

40

"No matter how many deny it, it's possible, probable, and quite likely that it will happen in the near future whether at your hands or the hands of someone else. Copernicus, Magellan, and the Wright Brothers are proof of that."

ACTION STEP

On a Venn diagram, compare and contrast some inventors/creators who lived before the eighteenth century with today's modern inventors/creators. Let each group occupy one circle, with the overlapping center representing what the two groups have in common. Focus on personality, professional attitude, attitude, or other directions that come to mind. Carefully diagram what they have in common as well as how they differ in regard to attitude.

1) _____

2) _____

3) _____

4) _____

5) _____

41

> *Just because you don't have wings doesn't mean you can't fly.*

ACTION STEP

Picture yourself as an inventor or creator. Describe what a day in your life would be like, what you might invent or create, some of the challenges that might come your way, and how you would meet those obstacles.

1) _____

2) _____

3) _____

4) _____

5) _____

42

Billions and billions of people throughout history thought man could never fly. Now we fly faster and higher than any other creature with wings.

ACTION STEP

Imagine going back in time two hundred years and attempting to explain flying in terms of modern technology. Give ten examples of how you might explain. How do you think people would react, and why?

1) _____

2) _____

3) _____

4) _____

5) _____

43

> *To foolishly believe something that has never been fully attempted is assumption, a very close relative of ignorance.*

ACTION STEP

Think of an event/time in your life when you wanted something (dating someone, securing a dream job, rebuilding a lost friendship) and you based your beliefs on assumptions rather than taking action. Create a cause/event/effects graph to probe the origins of these beliefs and their effects.

1) _____

2) _____

3) _____

4) _____

5) _____

44

> Play Punch Buggy every now and then. See a Volkswagen, punch the person next to you, and yell, "Punch buggy, no backsies!"— It's fun!

ACTION STEP

Name three ways in which you can incorporate silliness into your life, and five people who might benefit from it.

1) _____

2) _____

3) _____

45

There is something to be said for the world of play, a world most adults seem to have abandoned.

ACTION STEP

Thinking back to your childhood, list ten games you played. On a scale of one to ten, rate how those games better prepared you for the real world.

1) _____

2) _____

3) _____

4) _____

5) _____

46

In losing sight of the importance of play, most adults don't realize they also lose the majority of their creativity.

ACTION STEP

List ten games you played as a child and rate their creativity from one to five.

1) _____

2) _____

3) _____

4) _____

5) _____

6) _____

7) _____

8) _____

9) _____

10) _____

47

Growing up, we always want to make our own decisions. When we become adults, we gain responsibility and the decisions that go with it... and long for the days when we didn't have to make decisions.

ACTION STEP

If you magically transformed into your childhood self again, list the five things you would do differently or appreciate more the second time around.

1) _____

2) _____

3) _____

4) _____

5) _____

48

If we stopped looking at the other side of the fence, we would have a deeper appreciation for what we have growing in our own backyards.

ACTION STEP

List twenty things you have that others might wish they had. Prioritize them from most to least important.

1) _____

2) _____

3) _____

4) _____

5) _____

6) _____

7) _____

8) _____

9) _____

10) _____

49

If you feel a sudden desire to impact someone in a positive way, don't spend a lifetime trying to come up with fancy information—physical, emotional, professional, personal, spiritual, or otherwise. Just try laughter—simple, to the point, and contagious.

ACTION STEP

Go out of your way today to make ten people laugh. Tomorrow, try to make it eleven. Get competitive by constantly trying to top the previous day's amount.

1) _____

2) _____

3) _____

4) _____

5) _____

50

People have a natural desire to feel important and special, whether personally or professionally. Take the time to make those around you feel special.

ACTION STEP

Whether it's through your time, money, or effort, connect with three people who could benefit from your help.

1) _____

2) _____

3) _____

51

Recognize the uniqueness of people and voice it to them. Despite what may be obvious to you and so many others, people often find it difficult to see their own incredible qualities and the potential within themselves.

ACTION STEP

On a Frayer diagram, chart four classes of people; those you feel are above you, those you view as your peers, those you view as below you, and those who are complete strangers. List three people who fall into each category and think of three compliments you can pay each of them. Repeat the process often, and note the changes that take place in your life, both externally and internally.

1) _____

2) _____

3) _____

52

When in doubt, give yourself some homework. It may sound childish, but the basic premise of homework is to reinforce a lesson learned.

ACTION STEP

Think of four life lessons you had to repeat because you had forgotten them over time. Had you constantly kept them fresh in your mind, would you have needed to relearn them? Why or why not?

1) _____

2) _____

3) _____

4) _____

53

We continue growing throughout our lives with each passing day. New lessons are constantly thrust upon us. Why in the world wouldn't we reinforce the lessons we already learned? Find some homework... and do it!

ACTION STEP

Consider four challenges you have met in the past year, the hurdles they brought with them, and the lessons they provided. What could you have done after each lesson to further reinforce your constant awareness of the lesson?

1) _____

2) _____

3) _____

4) _____

54

There is nothing as beautiful as nature, and yet it's completely free. The next time your shoulders feel heavy with burden, look to the surrounding trees and let their boughs cradle your burdens.

ACTION STEP

Spend time with a tree; visually take in its immense size, proportion, and various parts. Listen to the sounds of the leaves rustling as the breeze blows through them. Smell the bark and the leaves. Completely take it in, and let it take you away.

1) _____

2) _____

3) _____

4) _____

55

The rosebush is the greatest example of what life truly is like. When you carefully take it in with your eyes, you see the beauty within it. When you carefully approach it, you can appreciate that beauty on a greater scale with multiple senses. But when you leap at it carelessly, the thorns will stick you.

ACTION STEP

Take an afternoon and smell roses.

1) _____

2) _____

3) _____

4) _____

5) _____

56

> Sadly, the thorns of a rosebush can remain in a person, seen as a terrible experience with nothing to be gained. In reality, thorns from a rosebush are lessons to be learned, much like the lessons life places in our way.

ACTION STEP

Review the most important lessons life has offered you and evaluate any "thorns" that may have accompanied them. Did you notice the thorns at the time? Now that you do notice them, do you see the connection between them and the lesson life offered you?

1) _____

2) _____

3) _____

4) _____

5) _____

57

Mirrors were created not to see the exterior appearance, but to better understand the soul through facial expressions and body language.

ACTION STEP

For five full minutes, study yourself in a mirror. Take note not just of your physical appearance, but of the slightest details within your facial expressions, posture, body language, etc. At the end of five minutes, log every detail you noticed about yourself physically (lines in the face, hairline, etc.), as well as similarities to those close to you (Do you look like your father? Mother? Sibling?). Log thoughts and emotions you had during the exercise as well, and what brought about those thoughts and emotions.

1) _____

2) _____

3) _____

4) _____

5) _____

58

Nothing places a mind in the direction of purpose, power, and energy more than a list of checked-off accomplishments

ACTION STEP

Imagine listing ten tasks that could be accomplished in five minutes or less, then doing them all within the next hour, checking each one off one by one. After only an hour, you will have a list of pure accomplishment.

1) _____

2) _____

3) _____

4) _____

5) _____

6) _____

7) _____

8) _____

9) _____

10) _____

59

When you're feeling tainted in your attitude toward life, take a moment and look at it through the eyes of a child. They delight in life with a sense of wonder. Reattach yourself to that sense of wonder by seeing the world as they do.

ACTION STEP

Take an hour or two out of your day and spend it with a child in your life. If you don't have a child in your life, visit a setting such as a children's museum or children's section of a library to gain an understanding of what appeals to them, how they see the world, and how they impact it.

1) _____

2) _____

3) _____

4) _____

5) _____

60

Pencils come with erasers for a reason. Don't just erase the mistake, though. Learn from it first and consider how that same space might be used again, this time with the correct answer.

ACTION STEP

Mistakes are our best tools for gaining wisdom, thus making them "our favorite mistakes". List ten of your favorite mistakes and brainstorm the best methods of fixing them for maximum learning potential.

1) _____

2) _____

3) _____

4) _____

5) _____

6) _____

7) _____

8) _____

9) _____

10) _____

61

I would rather seem strange in the eyes of others and be happy than conform to others' standards and remain miserable.

ACTION STEP

Describe at length a time in your life when you dared to stand out from the crowd. How did you feel? What kind of impact, if any, did it have on the people around you?

1) _____

2) _____

3) _____

4) _____

5) _____

62

It's amazing that the people who enter our lives at the beginning letting us know we can be or do whatever we want in life end up becoming the first ones to stress our need to conform to the ways of society and brag of our conformed achievements to their friends and family.

ACTION STEP

Using a Fraher diagram, place three people from your early years in the center diamond. In the upper left corner, write the occupations/things you wanted to be when you grew up. In the upper right corner, list the ways those three people reacted to these goals. In the lower left corner, list the lofty goals and desires you had as you grew older, and write the corresponding reactions in the bottom right corner. Compare the reactions to those of your younger years. How have these reactions impacted you and your goal setting over time?

1) _____

2) _____

3) _____

63

We spend so much time doing as we're told, following the right and wrong laid down to us by others (family, friends, bosses) that it never dawns on us to ask if they truly are the be-all and end-all on the subject of right and wrong.
We believe blindly.

ACTION STEP

With the help of a partner, blindfold yourself and allow the partner to be your eyes for thirty minutes. Go about your business as you normally would. At the end of the exercise, carefully evaluate how much you questioned the partner's reliability at the start of the exercise versus the end of it.

1) _____

2) _____

3) _____

4) _____

5) _____

64

When no credence is given to the journey and all value is placed on the destination, we—like a horse wearing blinders—miss much of what is going on in the world around us.

ACTION STEP

Take a walk and be sure to focus only on the destination. Take a second walk on the same path without focusing on the destination, but rather on the journey itself, taking in as much of it as possible. Finally, take a third walk with no destination in mind at all. Compare and contrast the similarities and differences between the three walks. What benefits did you gain in the three different cases?

1) _____

2) _____

3) _____

4) _____

5) _____

65

Welcome to the world of entitlement, where most of the people complaining that life isn't fair have more time, money, and material possessions than the people who feel life is fair.

ACTION STEP

Create a table with three columns and ten rows. Let the columns reflect time, money, and effort (convenience). In the spaces beneath the title, list ways in which *your* life has become much easier compared to either those around you or those in other countries. List these in the areas of time, finance, and comfort/convenience/ease.

66

A squirrel stores nuts for the coming winter. It makes the time when the right season approaches and all else goes on the back burner because of the importance of preparation.

ACTION STEP

Research three fables that deal with the topic of preparation. How did the fable end for each character based on how they prepared? Create your own fable using animals as characters and place people from your life in the story.

1) _____

2) _____

3) _____

67

Animals do; they don't reason. They take action, make mistakes, adapt, and do it again. Such is learning; such is the path to achievement.

ACTION STEP

Either in person or through a video, watch a newborn animal try to walk. Take particular notice of how the animal reacts when it falls, as well as how the mother reacts on instinct rather than logic or reason.

1) _____

2) _____

3) _____

68

Multitasking is limited—that is why people who put all their energy into thinking are unable to successfully do.

ACTION STEP

Write a newly created list of things to do on scraps of paper. List them in order of priority. Keep the first task in hand. Crumple up all the other papers and throw them in the garbage, one at a time. Shoot for distance, making a game out of it. As you release each task from your hand, release it from your mind as well.

1) _____

2) _____

3) _____

4) _____

5) _____

69

There is a direct correlation between supply and demand. This also applies to perceived supply and perceived demand. The more unavailable something is, the more it's desired, whether it's needed or not.

ACTION STEP

On a Frayer diagram, use one corner to list your monetary possessions; a second to list the monetary things recently received, a third to list the monetary things you still want, and the fourth for the intangibles you already possess. Compare and contrast the corners, pondering these key questions:

  i. Once you obtain something, how much do you still desire it?
  ii. How much desire do you have for the intangible things?
  iii. Do you desire the intangible as much as the tangible?
  iv. Why or why not?

1) _____

2) _____

3) _____

4) _____

5) _____

70

Combine two things in a way they have never been combined before and three things will happen: 1) You will have created something new; 2) It will have some kind of purpose, whether that purpose is realized by you or someone else; 3) People will line up to have it.

ACTION STEP

List thirteen everyday objects you have around the house. How can you change the shape, color, form, pattern, etc., to make them different than you've ever seen before? How could two or more be combined to create something new? What kind of purpose could this new item serve? Who would it best serve?

1) _____
2) _____
3) _____
4) _____
5) _____
6) _____
7) _____
8) _____
9) _____
10) _____
11) _____
12) _____
13) _____

71

You start learning the moment you draw your first breath and continue learning until you draw your last. Since learning, like exercise, takes up time, why wouldn't we give it equal time or care? Develop knowledge awareness.

ACTION STEP

Take one hour of your day to drive unfamiliar streets. Realize how you notice things along the way: houses, gardens, children, etc. Now return to streets you drive frequently and apply the same awareness. After an hour, list twenty-five things you noticed that you never took notice of before.

1) _____

2) _____

3) _____

4) _____

5) _____

6) _____

7) _____

8) _____

9) _____

10) _____

72

It was once thought by millions that the world was flat, our planet was the center of the universe, and demons lived among us. Despite how many people believe something, it can still be wrong.

ACTION STEP

Create a list of seven people in history who were misunderstood and mocked for their beliefs. Give consideration to those same historically widespread beliefs (such as the world being flat and the universe rotating around the earth). Briefly write about what the world may be like today if early thinkers *didn't* have the determination to support their own beliefs despite so many people believing otherwise.

1) _____

2) _____

3) _____

4) _____

5) _____

6) _____

7) _____

73

> *I would rather die trying to help someone than live knowing I helped no one. The latter is a long and lonely existence at best.*

ACTION STEP

For seven days, go out of your way to help as many people as you can. At the end of seven days, make a three-column table. In the first column, list the benefits you provided in each instance; in the second column, record people's reactions to your help; and in the final column, list how you felt after you helped each time.

1) _____

2) _____

3) _____

4) _____

5) _____

6) _____

7) _____

74

> Money mind-set is the greatest destroyer of positive energy.

ACTION STEP

Write of a time when pursuing money cost you something much more important, and share the lesson learned as a result. Otherwise, list fifteen purchases made in the past year that you felt you needed. On a scale of one to eight, rate their importance as compared to the things in your life that are God-given—freedom of speech, love, liberty, happiness, health, relationships, romance, achievement, etc.

1) _____

2) _____

3) _____

4) _____

5) _____

6) _____

7) _____

8) _____

9) _____

10) _____

75

By first tackling the project we least want to do, we achieve a greater sense of accomplishment and ease the way in accomplishing tasks throughout the rest of the day.

ACTION STEP

Give three examples of big projects that needed resolved (home repair, for example) that you procrastinated. List any negative consequences that resulted.

1) _____

2) _____

3) _____

76

Personal wealth is comprised of many components, including but not limited to personal health, productivity, and positive relationships; but there's no room in personal wealth for money.

ACTION STEP

Write a children's story conveying the importance of personal wealth. Include characters striving to achieve happiness, self-assuredness, and contentment. Be sure to include a character who focuses on internal gifts and a character who focuses only on money. Make sure the right character gets the "happily ever after."

1) _____

2) _____

3) _____

4) _____

5) _____

77

The more you run desperately toward something, the less likely your chance of connecting with it. The less you look in its direction, the greater the chance it will come to you.

ACTION STEP

Spend one hour contemplating the kind of people you want to attract in your life. Visualize every trait about them and write as much detail as possible. Then, rather than look for people displaying those qualities, *be* that person and see the reactions from those around you. Log the differences with each passing day.

1) _____

2) _____

3) _____

4) _____

5) _____

78

Passion plus pursuit produces perfection. Everything aligns for success.

ACTION STEP

Create a K.W.L. chart. In the "K(now)" column, lists the things you know you are passionate about. Under the "W(ant to know)" column, list the pursuits you believe tie both directly and indirectly to your passion. Under the "L(earn)" column, list what you learn once you apply your passions with action in the direction you believe would benefit others.

1) _____

2) _____

3) _____

4) _____

5) _____

79

When all seeds are planted at once, no seeds receive the necessary time, space, or TLC needed to ensure complete growth. It is no different with people.

ACTION STEP

Plant a seed and take care of it daily. Measure and log its progress each day over four to six weeks. Then "plant your own seeds"—write three tasks you want to achieve, and work on them daily for the next thirty days. Measure and log your own progress as you did the seed's. How do they compare?

1) _____

2) _____

3) _____

4) _____

5) _____

80

The farmer is the best teacher; harvesting vegetables requires the same skill as harvesting potential.

ACTION STEP

Create a tall tale about a farmer who harvests ideas as crops instead of fruits and vegetables. What might some of his ideas be? Who would they benefit? How might he benefit in return?

1) _____

2) _____

3) _____

4) _____

5) _____

81

The one who puts off the task of greater priority accomplishes much less and does so with little efficiency, since his mind remains consumed with the task he dreads.

ACTION STEP

Consider five large tasks you pushed off in the past year and the results of the procrastination. Questions to ponder;

  i. Did procrastination benefit or hinder your progress?
  ii. What benefits or hindrances resulted?
  iii. Had you completed the task on time, how could you have benefited?
  iv. How might you have benefited if you had attacked the task with a vengeance?
  v. How could others have benefitted from early or on-time task completion?

1) _____

2) _____

3) _____

4) _____

5) _____

82

Whether on the edge of a riverbed or in a tin cup, the seed pushes its roots firmly down and its flower up toward the light. Environment plays a small part when potential develops.

ACTION STEP

Plant two seeds in different environments; one in a cup and one in the ground. Let the seed in the cup receive water and food. Give the seed in the ground nothing. Write journal entries on the progress of the two seeds, and consider how this compares to nourishing a dream. Compare the seed in the cup to the nourished dream and the seed in the ground to the unnourished dream. What role do the plant food and water play in the role of the dreams? What is the difference between the two kinds of dreams and why? Will the unnourished dream survive? Why? What action can you take to change that?

1) _____

2) _____

3) _____

4) _____

5) _____

83

All the horsepower in the world will get you nowhere if there's no traction between the tires and the road.

ACTION STEP

Write down some real-life examples of people failing to accomplish things because they didn't take the proper steps to get started, build momentum, and sustain the task to completion. As you write, focus on the end results—the emotional impact and the impact on the decision-making process toward other tasks. Focus as well on what these people could have done differently to gain traction (organizing, focusing, benefitting others, etc.). Write a one-page paper on your observations entitled, "The Important Thing is…" Start the paper with this phrase and focus on what's important within the noted failures and means of remedy.

1) _____

2) _____

3) _____

4) _____

5) _____

84

Value increases exponentially as a person drastically increases the number of creative or unique skills provided to a given niche.

ACTION STEP

Create two triangles with three levels in each. Draw the first triangle upside down and the second triangle right side up. Label the first triangle "skills/gifts" and the second one "career/purpose." Starting at the bottom level, list the kinds of skills/gifts you have, and in the bottom part of the second triangle write the kind of career or purpose to which it would apply. Narrow the selection more specifically in the second triangle at the middle level. Narrow it even further at the top level. Now look to the first triangle and determine which skills and talents would best suit reaching those niched areas and organize a means by which you will acquire them.

1) _____

2) _____

3) _____

4) _____

5) _____

85

Horse-drawn carriages have blind spots, cars have blind spots, even airplanes have blind spots. Anything in motion toward a destination has a blind spot. Beware the blind spot.

ACTION STEP

List eight goals you have had in the past two years. Rate their importance on a scale of one to ten. List an obstacle for each, and on a scale of one to ten, rate the challenges they presented to your achievement. Now list eight upcoming goals and the kinds of obstacles that might present themselves. What kind of rating might they have on the scale?

1) _____

2) _____

3) _____

4) _____

5) _____

6) _____

7) _____

8) _____

86

Blind spots are the world's way of checking to make sure you're paying attention.

ACTION STEP

Tape pieces of construction paper to the sides of your head, similar to a horse's blinders. Spend five minutes walking around the house, park, etc. Remove the blinders and take the same walk. Take note of everything you now see to the sides of you that you didn't before. How does this compare to the challenges life presents you as you set out to achieve your goals?

1) _____

2) _____

3) _____

4) _____

5) _____

87

Taking control of your life begins with taking control of your emotions.

ACTION STEP

Write a letter to yourself in the future. Discuss some of the choices that you made solely out of emotion and how they affected your life. Apologize for the bad choices your future self must now contend with and come up with ideas for how the situations may be resolved.

1) _____

2) _____

3) _____

4) _____

5) _____

88

Celebrities need dogs like anyone else because like everyone in this world, they require someone or something in their lives to show them compassion and unconditional love no matter what goes on around them. Surround yourself with those who love you, and embrace their love and compassion.

ACTION STEP

List the ten people closest to you. Give careful thought to their level of support, love, and compassion, and rate it on a scale of one to eight. Should you allow other people to get closer to you that would rate higher?

1) _____

2) _____

3) _____

4) _____

5) _____

6) _____

7) _____

8) _____

9) _____

10) _____

89

The difference between dogs and cats is their direction of attitude; Cats have an internal direction (putting themselves first), while dogs have an external direction (putting others first). Because of man's ability to reason, we need to embody a blend of both.

ACTION STEP

Create a three-column chart. Beside it, list ten historical figures. In the first column next to each figure, state the action or event for which he or she is known; in the second column, state how that action benefited him or her (internal); in the third, state how that action benefited others (external).

90

People need to understand their need to make themselves happy by first finding what they're passionate about, and then serving others using that passion.

ACTION STEP

Using index cards, write down activities or items you come across in everyday travels that bring a smile to your face. Next to it, write down any pursuits that the activity could be used towards. On each, skip a line and write how you might use that pursuit to benefit someone else in some way. Keep the cards close to you and be sure to look back at them on a regular basis. As new passions arise, add them to new cards and list new people who you might benefit from your passions.

1) _____

2) _____

3) _____

4) _____

5) _____

91

> The nemesis of success is micromanagement.

ACTION STEP

Create a Venn diagram with the first circle representing a micromanaged group and the second representing a group empowered to take initiative. Let any qualities that apply to both go in the center area where both circles overlap. Carefully examine the similarities and the differences.

1) _____

2) _____

3) _____

4) _____

5) _____

92

Employees who are told by an employer how to do every little task within their jobs experience a decreased opportunity to be creative or put a part of themselves into the task, eliminating their desire to do it at all.

ACTION STEP

Think of a class or job you had at some point in your life where every task was under a figurative microscope. How did it make you feel to have no input into a task you were performing? As time progressed, did you feel more or less empowered?

1) _____

2) _____

3) _____

4) _____

5) _____

93

Just because others don't see your thoughts or actions as amazing now doesn't mean you aren't way ahead of the curve or that you won't be appreciated ten or twenty years from now. The most influential people were seen as pathetic crackpots in their own time. The truth is, the world requires time to catch up with genius.

ACTION STEP

Consider a time in your life when you firmly believed in something but others discouraged you. Did you listen to them? If so, did it benefit or hinder your attitude?

1) _____

2) _____

3) _____

4) _____

5) _____

94

The best thing for a child to do is make a mistake and learn from it. The hardest thing for a parent to do is allow that very mistake.

ACTION STEP

Think of a common mistake most children make that you have made yourself (stealing a candy bar, for example). Think about how the mistake impacted you as a child, and your parents' response to it. Now consider how you have responded as a parent when your child made that very same mistake. Could you have done something to better prepare your child and prevent it, or was it something he or she had to learn independently? Did that hold true when *you* made the mistake? Journal about this and about how you feel as a parent knowing your children will probably need to experience mistakes and failure firsthand to better learn the lessons. How does this make you feel as a parent?

1) _____

2) _____

3) _____

4) _____

5) _____

95

Sometimes the trail that reconnects you with your imagination must start with a trail of breadcrumbs that takes you back in time.

ACTION STEP

Observe children either around you or through video, and watch their interactions with their environment. Take note of how they use their imaginations in regard to their environment and their situations. Write a field report based on your observations.

1) _____

2) _____

3) _____

4) _____

5) _____

96

Time doesn't really heal wounds; it gives us the opportunity to make newer mistakes that we must focus on instead.

ACTION STEP

List five points in your life where you made large mistakes and consider the length of time it took to heal. What entered your life at that point, and how much of your focus was on the large mistake? What obstacles posed themselves at this point that caused you to focus less on the larger mistake?

1) _____

2) _____

3) _____

4) _____

5) _____

97

> *The more the mouth lies, the more truth rests within the eyes.*

ACTION STEP

List seven different forms of nonverbal communication that you can count on to reveal a person in the moments when they lie.

1) _____

2) _____

3) _____

4) _____

5) _____

6) _____

7) _____

98

Benefiting from mistakes is a means of leveraging our learning curve.

ACTION STEP

Consider seven important mistakes in your life. At the time, did you consider them positive or negative? What did you gain from experiencing those failures? If seen in a positive light rather than a negative one, how much more could you have learned, and how much more could you have benefited?

1) _____

2) _____

3) _____

4) _____

5) _____

6) _____

7) _____

99

Wealth is any given person's means of measuring his or her success in life, plain and simple.

ACTION STEP

Give eight examples of wealth that have nothing to do with money. For each one, give an example of how many people benefit from it.

1) _____

2) _____

3) _____

4) _____

5) _____

6) _____

7) _____

8) _____

100

The hardest problems are always the internal ones for which we seek an external answer; in reality, the answer—like the question—rests solely within us.

ACTION STEP

Think of the most successful points in your life (meeting the person you love, graduating college, getting a promotion, becoming a parent for the first time, etc.) and consider the kind of person you were at that point. Rate your confidence during each of those moments and some of the things that gave you great confidence.

1) _____

2) _____

3) _____

4) _____

5) _____

6) _____

7) _____

8) _____

101

Little good comes when drinking from a fire hose. Overloading in any focused area can be as unproductive as trying to focus in various directions all at once.

ACTION STEP

Detail five tasks you would like to accomplish. Try to get them all done at the same time within the same day. Document your progress and efficiency with each task. Then take on just one task, such as starting a business, taking a course, or reconnecting with a significant other, and attempt to overload the amount you would do in a given day. Document the progress and efficiency of this as well. Using a Venn diagram, demonstrate the two styles and compare and contrast them.

1) _____

2) _____

3) _____

4) _____

5) _____

102

We always seem to meet people who have more questions than answers. Forget the man who has all the answers—I want to meet the man who has more questions than answers, because he'll still have a few leftover questions should there ever be a need.

ACTION STEP

Spend your day finding three people who often ask good questions. Start following the model they set for you and set out each day to ask three good questions of your own, seeking the answers as you go along.

1) _____

2) _____

3) _____

4) _____

5) _____

103

> He made the platypus just in case we started thinking we had all the answers.

ACTION STEP

For every rule there is an exception. Think about the seahorse, for example, where the male gives birth to the young and takes care of them in the early stages rather than the mother. How would such an exception impact people? Using a computer, research and list eight examples in nature that serve as the exception to the rule. Once completed, briefly describe each example, its exception, and how you think it would affect people if that exception were one we had to deal with.

1) _____

2) _____

3) _____

4) _____

5) _____

6) _____

7) _____

8) _____

104

I'm getting tired of celebrating Columbus Day; he discovered a place already inhabited. That's like me walking down Main Street in Disney World and placing my flag in the ground, claiming it in the name of Leo.

ACTION STEP

List seven people who have received more credit than they may have deserved. Now give thought to some of your own achievements. Sometimes it helps to focus more on the humanity in others in order to recognize our own potential in moments of doubt.

1) _____

2) _____

3) _____

4) _____

5) _____

6) _____

7) _____

105

> Some of the most celebrated people may not have really achieved as much as history gives them credit for, and those who have reached achievement did so with a great deal of failure along the way.

ACTION STEP

Diagram in the manner of your choosing eleven discoverers/inventors. List their noted accomplishments, then research and list everything it took them to get there.

1) _____

2) _____

3) _____

4) _____

5) _____

106

Guided intelligence is expertise. Misguided intelligence becomes the humorous writings of Mark Twain.

ACTION STEP

On the computer, find a list of quotes from Mark Twain. Read them and briefly write not only about the wisdom within them, but about the tone as well. What is the overarching point behind the majority of his quotes?

1) _____

2) _____

3) _____

4) _____

5) _____

107

A microphone in the right hands is power; a microphone in the wrong hands may as well be a paperweight.

ACTION STEP

Communication is one of the most powerful tools a person can wield, assuming they know how to properly communicate. List 7 seven areas of communication that most people can improve upon and name seven areas of life where communication plays a major role.

1) _____

2) _____

3) _____

4) _____

5) _____

6) _____

7) _____

108

A good joke doesn't make the problem go away, it makes the worry go away, enabling you to finally solve the problem.

ACTION STEP

Research the healing power of humor. Classify four ways in which it can lead to a healthier lifestyle.

1) _____

2) _____

3) _____

4) _____

109

When it comes to quotes, I am no Mark Twain, but many may have said the same about him in his time.

ACTION STEP

Write three new quotes a day for thirty days. At the end of the month, compare your quotes from the beginning of the month to those at the end. What kind of patterns or changes did you notice? Compare them to quotes from recognized people in history. How do they compare?

1) _____

2) _____

3) _____

110

Truth be told, peanut butter and jelly don't really go together as readily as others would have you believe.

ACTION STEP

Summarize some examples of paired items perceived as "going together" that you have been taught growing up. Did you pass these perceptions on to others, and if so, on what facts did you base these perceptions?

1) _____

2) _____

3) _____

4) _____

5) _____

6) _____

7) _____

8) _____

111

> Conspiracy theories are nothing more than a conspiracy theory.

ACTION STEP

Just for fun, create a conspiracy theory. Focus either on a famous event in history or focus on a specific event within your own life. What kind of theory would you create, and how far-fetched would it be? What reasoning might lead to creating it?

1) _____

2) _____

3) _____

4) _____

5) _____

112

> Dreams are meant to be chased...why else would you have legs?

ACTION STEP

Write a list of every dream you have ever had since you were a child. How many have you realized? How many did you fall short of achieving? Why?

1) _____

2) _____

3) _____

4) _____

5) _____

6) _____

7) _____

8) _____

113

In order to find what you seek "out there," you must first look deep inside.

ACTION STEP

Consider a time when you experienced heartache. How did you get beyond it? How did you regain control of your thoughts in order to move forward with your life?

1) _____

2) _____

3) _____

4) _____

5) _____

6) _____

7) _____

8) _____

114

The difference between doors and windows is time; windows are open for a time and then closed whether we like it or not. Doors, on the other hand are always within our grasp. We just have to turn the knob and give a little push.

ACTION STEP

How many times in the past year have you let a window close on an opportunity? How many doors have you persisted in opening? Did you manage to grab opportunities in time before the window closed, or did you put in the effort to open the door? If so, did you feel a sense of achievement? Summarize these answers in a paragraph.

1) _____

2) _____

3) _____

4) _____

5) _____

115

Everything starts small. Nourishment is the difference between something living or dying, flourishing or starving.

ACTION STEP

On a Frayer diagram, list four things that require nourishment to grow (consider including people as one of these items). List the many different kinds of nourishment, the results of the nourishment, and how the lack of nourishment impacts the outcome.

1) _____

2) _____

3) _____

4) _____

116

We have four basic needs in this world; food, shelter, clothing, and love. Interesting that the most important one is the only intangible one.

ACTION STEP

List five intangibles you possess that you take for granted besides love.

1) _____

2) _____

3) _____

4) _____

5) _____

117

> The difference between joy and sorrow is the difference between the journey and the destination. The first offers much on its way somewhere… the other offers only an arrival.

ACTION STEP

We often see joy as an arrival point rather than a sustainable emotion. We are often able to hold onto sorrow for a longer period due to our ability to think about it for an extended period of time. Compile a list of ten points in your life when you experienced joy and ten points when you experienced sorrow. Give an idea of how long the emotion lasted in each case. Which, for the most part, lasted longer? Why? In situations where joy arises, what can be done to hold onto it longer? What can be done to turn a situation of sorrow to a situation of joy?

1) _____

2) _____

3) _____

4) _____

5) _____

118

> Destinations are at most, only a point of arrival. I've never seen a child look forward to going to Disney World just for the arrival in the parking lot.

ACTION STEP

Create a three column chart with the words destination, journey, and lesson in each column respectively. Choose five physical destinations you look forward to visiting. If possible, go back and drive to those destinations again, this time focusing on the journey instead of the destination. What differences do you notice this time? Write down those differences and what you can learn from them, then further expound on this new way of looking at journeys and destinations.

1) _____

2) _____

3) _____

4) _____

5) _____

119

> *If you don't believe in yourself, no one else will have a reason to.*

ACTION STEP

Choose five physical exercises that prove difficult for you. Do them diligently, and monitor yourself to see how many you can do, how much weight you can lift, how your muscle tone changes, etc. Take written notes not just of the physical changes but of your attitude toward yourself as well.

1) _____

2) _____

3) _____

4) _____

5) _____

120

Good music is not heard, it is felt. We do not need to understand the words or its purpose; only the purpose it serves us internally.

ACTION STEP

A song can appeal to masses, but how it appeals to the individual has to do with the individual's experiences. Give an example of three songs that connect with you, and explore why. What makes these songs so special over the thousands of others that exist? What personal experiences make these songs connect with you?

1) _____

2) _____

3) _____

4) _____

5) _____

121

> To me, faith is believing in something without needing proof.

ACTION STEP

Give six examples in your life that called for faith or a need to turn to a higher power. Did such moments call for prayer? Did the prayers work? Did praying prove cathartic and healing for you? If not, what could have been done differently to reach the needed healing?

1) _____

2) _____

3) _____

4) _____

5) _____

6) _____

122

Ironically, vision requires a closing of the eyes in order to truly open them.

ACTION STEP

Consider four different points in your life that called for vision (ages seven, fifteen, twenty-two, and thirty-five, for example). During each time, list what you wanted to do with your life and how you visualized yourself *being* that thing.

1) _____

2) _____

3) _____

4) _____

123

Audacity is having the nerve to hold others to a standard that we, ourselves, cannot attain.

ACTION STEP

Think of three separate times in your life when you may have expected more from others because of their age or your relationship to them (parents, for example). Create a three-column chart stating 1) what you thought, 2) what you did, and 3) what you could have done instead.

1) _____

2) _____

3) _____

124

The probability of achievement is directly proportionate to the duration of perseverance.

ACTION STEP

Consider five times in your life when you failed to achieve what you set out to. It can be anything from securing a job to asking someone out on a date. Had you stuck it out rather than thrown in the towel, is it possible you may have finally achieved what you desired? If so, how much more effort would it have taken on your part? How could this difference have impacted your life from that point forward?

1) _____

2) _____

3) _____

4) _____

5) _____

125

> In the wake of tragedy comes an awareness of our inner strengths.

ACTION STEP

Using a flowchart, chart an occasion where your luck seemed to have taken a severe turn for the worse. Demonstrate how each problem resulted in something more and where the end result (and lesson) finally left you.

1) _____

2) _____

3) _____

4) _____

5) _____

126

> To wake and breathe is all we need for a good day.

ACTION STEP

When you wake, rather than follow through on your daily morning rituals, stop and count how many blessings you have in your life. Try to turn this into your new daily ritual.

1) _____

2) _____

3) _____

4) _____

5) _____

127

> The greatest mountain to be scaled lies not outside, but within.

ACTION STEP

Consider a time when you were your own worst enemy and posed the biggest obstacle to your own progress toward goals. Create an outline demonstrating what those goals were, and how you got in your own way. If at all possible, also create a section of the outline demonstrating the steps you took to get out of your own way. If you have never been in such a situation, speak to someone who has and outline their goals, obstacles, and resolution.

1) _____

2) _____

3) _____

4) _____

5) _____

128

Words are merely thoughts verbalized. Control of thoughts is the key to communication.

ACTION STEP

Create a Frayer diagram and label four separate categories "What I thought," "What I said," "What I *should* have said," and "What the outcome *could* have been." Consider three occasions when you said something to someone without giving consideration to the outcome. Apply these three occasions to each category.

1) _____

2) _____

3) _____

4) _____

129

| Achievement is potential unleashed! |

ACTION STEP

Using a Frayer diagram, create four categories labeled "Desired outcome," "Results of outcome," "Emotions," and "Return on achievement." Choose three occasions when you were persistent to a point of accomplishment. Write the three desired outcomes, the results, how you felt emotionally upon achievement, and how you either paid it forward or had it positively come back to you.

1) _____

2) _____

3) _____

4) _____

130

> *Visualize achievement and take action.*

ACTION STEP

Spend five minutes a day in darkness and silence. Give yourself a place without distraction and practice the art of visualization. Start small, visualizing the things you see around you just before closing your eyes. As you progress in your level of comfort, start moving the images in your mind from the things you see to the things you *desire*. Be sure to be deliberate in your process and see the images all the way through to achievement. In time, progress your images to the long-term goals you desire rather than the short-term goals.

1) _____

2) _____

3) _____

4) _____

5) _____

131

> I have all I need to be successful: an awareness that life's lessons are always surrounding me, ready to be learned.

ACTION STEP

Pay careful attention to every detail of the events that happen around you today. Take careful note of any patterns along the way. Write a list of the life lessons offered this day, as well as what helped you notice them today as opposed to any other day.

1) _____

2) _____

3) _____

4) _____

5) _____

132

> We learn, we share, and we continue the life lesson through teaching.

ACTION STEP

Take three life lessons you have learned this past year and share them with three other people in your life. How did teaching them what you learned through personal experience benefit them? How did it benefit you? Did you receive anything else in return?

1) _____

2) _____

3) _____

133

I have nothing but respect for the man who will go to all lengths to take care of his family.

ACTION STEP

Briefly describe in written form the sacrifices you have made for your family and how they have benefited as a result. How did you benefit physically, mentally, and emotionally?

1) _____

2) _____

3) _____

4) _____

5) _____

GET QUOTIVATED!

134

> Given the chance, positive energy will always preside.

ACTION STEP

For one day, pattern your behavior in a negative direction in regard to your thoughts, words, and actions. The next day, pattern yourself with positive words, thoughts, and actions. Chart the results on a cause/events/effects diagram and review the differences between the two approaches.

1) _____

2) _____

3) _____

4) _____

5) _____

135

> We are the culmination of our successes and failures, each an open book from which others can learn.

ACTION STEP

On a Venn diagram, create two circles: one representing your failures and one your successes. Let the overlapping part represent the portion of your successes and failures that provide lessons from which others can learn.

1) _____

2) _____

3) _____

4) _____

5) _____

136

Scaling personal mountains is like reaching the end of the rainbow, only the pot of gold is internal.

ACTION STEP

Consider five obstacles in your life that you viewed as completely negative at the time. Imagine you are a hunter on safari. Observe these obstacles in their "natural habitats," writing a description of their characteristics (strengths and weaknesses) and laying out a plan for how you will capture each one. Conclude with the mounting of each head in your trophy room.

1) _____

2) _____

3) _____

4) _____

5) _____

137

Today's fortune cookie forecast: sunny with a strong chance of achievement.

ACTION STEP

Sometimes it becomes more important to take achievement, potential, and development in a lighter direction. Create a weather forecast for your goals and personal development. Be sure to include "a slight chance of (insert obstacle here)," concluding with a positive outcome. Be as descriptive as possible. Film yourself delivering your "weather report" for your personal development.

1) _____

2) _____

3) _____

4) _____

5) _____

138

It's such a small thing to see something from someone else's point of view, yet the positive impact is profound.

ACTION STEP

Consider the three most recent conflicts or differences of opinion you have shared with someone. Rather than taking your own side, try focusing all of your energy on seeing things his or her way. How could this benefit both of you as individuals? How might it benefit your relationship?

1) _____

2) _____

3) _____

4) _____

5) _____

139

Embrace the obstacles and hurdle them. They are life's greatest teachers.

ACTION STEP

Take a moment and list some of the largest obstacles you have encountered in your lifetime. Also, list how you became a better person as a result of them. Set them up in a rating chart, rating the size of the obstacles and the importance of the lessons from one to ten.

1) _____

2) _____

3) _____

4) _____

5) _____

140

> With regard to yesterday's mistakes, today is the opportunity for creating a better tomorrow.

ACTION STEP

Using a word web (a diagram allowing a word or phrase to be seen at the center and numerous other words or phrases stemming out from it - as seen in the diagram section in the rear of the book), diagram three hurdles from your past and demonstrate the aspects of your life that were impacted as a result. Include any changes that could have taken place in your life as well.

1) _____

2) _____

3) _____

4) _____

5) _____

141

> *The Mayans were pessimists! Life is just beginning!*

ACTION STEP

Spend a day looking for signs of life in the world. Travel to areas you normally don't travel in order to see the things you don't normally see. Write a brief letter or create a recording telling someone about what you saw and how it impacted you.

1) _____

2) _____

3) _____

4) _____

5) _____

142

Through attempts to better understand others, you will gain a greater understanding of yourself.

ACTION STEP

Ask fifteen people to list qualities that they feel best represent them, personality or otherwise. Create a rating scale listing all of those characteristics, and rate yourself on a scale of one to ten in each area. As a follow-up, give an example within your life that reinforces that rating.

1) _____

2) _____

3) _____

4) _____

5) _____

6) _____

7) _____

8) _____

143

Still standing!

ACTION STEP

Briefly describe three times in your life when you met tremendous adversity that should have stopped you, but instead made you stronger. Indicate in what areas of your life you became stronger as a result and how it impacted your life from that point forward.

1) _____

2) _____

3) _____

144

Pursuing your passion gives you your zest for life. Anything less is mundane.

ACTION STEP

Using a Venn diagram, create one circle listing your passions, both past and present. In the other circle, list all of the life roles and careers you have enjoyed. Be sure that the overlapping inner section represents the passions that match up with the life roles and careers.

1) _____

2) _____

3) _____

4) _____

5) _____

145

> The more creative the presentation of content, the more apt students are to learn it.

ACTION STEP

Create a chart demonstrating each of the five senses as well as two methods of learning for each sense. How can this chart be used to design a more enjoyable sense of learning for yourself? How can it be used to benefit others? If the method of learning were more enjoyable, what would you be more interested in learning more about? What methods would you use to creatively teach others what you already know?

1) _____

2) _____

3) _____

4) _____

5) _____

146

> *Laughter is the greatest joy.*

ACTION STEP

Create a list of various topics, movies, comedy shticks, routines, people, animals, etc., that make you laugh. On a scale of one to eight, rate the joy that each one brings you, and list how often you expose yourself to each. Are you getting enough laughter in your life?

1) _____

2) _____

3) _____

4) _____

5) _____

6) _____

7) _____

8) _____

147

> We are starry-eyed.

ACTION STEP

Take a night and stare at the stars. Using your imagination, create constellations of yourself at pivotal points in your life, both good and bad, that served as turning points in your development. Create a "constellation registry" where you not only get to create the constellation, but name it and write its backstory as well.

1) _____

2) _____

3) _____

4) _____

5) _____

6) _____

7) _____

8) _____

148

> Minute adjustments over time equal huge desired change.

ACTION STEP

Make a huge change in your life and try to sustain that change. A huge change would be something that severely disrupts the routine of daily life. Be sure that the change is something that is reversible (consider rental of something as an example of a huge reversible change). On a scale of one to eight, rate the difficulty you experience contending with the change each day. At the end of two weeks, stop the change and make a tiny change in your life. Rate the difficulty of that change on a scale of one to twelve. Compare the results. Which is more likely, over time, to create the desired end result?

1) _____

2) _____

3) _____

4) _____

5) _____

149

Actions don't just have a deadline; they have a birth line as well, a carefully planned starting point in alignment with the birth points of other activities going on at the same time.

ACTION STEP

Create your to-do list for the next few days. Rather than putting as much on the list as possible, create your list based on the amount of time in the day, the priority of each task, the size of each task, and the task deadline. Give careful thought to the task's starting time. Does it need to begin when it is originally placed on the to-do list, or can it be pushed off until a day is available that allows for more time? Try adjusting the starting point of all your tasks to allow for a reasonable time frame for each task.

1) _____

2) _____

3) _____

4) _____

5) _____

150

> When you help someone else discover his or her potential, you have discovered your own greatness.

ACTION STEP

Today, help five people discover, in some big or small way, that they are capable of far more than they realize. Answer the following questions:

  i. How did it make you feel?
  ii. Did you notice *you* were capable of doing more than you thought you could?
  iii. How did it make them feel?
  iv. How might they react the next time they face an obstacle?
  v. Will you pay this forward? Will they?

1) _____

2) _____

3) _____

4) _____

5) _____

151

The wisdom of your yesterday combined with the actions of today result in the achievements of tomorrow.

ACTION STEP

Think back to three things in your past you may have done differently had you possessed the knowledge you now have. If you had taken action based on that knowledge, where would it have lead you today? Log each example.

1) _____

2) _____

3) _____

4) _____

5) _____

152

It's not the size of the hurdle before you, or even your ability to safely get over it; it's your persistence in getting up that counts the most.

ACTION STEP

Write a mission statement for yourself dictating your commitment to persistence no matter what obstacles present themselves to you, your loved ones, or anyone with whom you come in contact.

1) _____

2) _____

3) _____

4) _____

5) _____

153

A life without challenge is a life not offering lessons, and therefore a life not worth living.

ACTION STEP

Find three of the most successful people in your community, business, or family. Rather than discuss their successes or achievements, interview them on their failures and ask them to discuss the vital role those failures and setbacks played in achieving the success they've known.

1) _____

2) _____

3) _____

154

> *If all the world's a stage, make your mark and steal the spotlight.*

ACTION STEP

Knowing every action you take can benefit someone, use today to benefit five people in as profound a manner as possible. Where possible, create an awareness of those benefits to the greater community around you.

1) _____

2) _____

3) _____

4) _____

5) _____

155

A picture's worth a thousand words; let others see what can be done, not only hear a dramatization.

ACTION STEP

List five examples of things we teach our children to do that we, ourselves, fail to do. Then carefully and truly model those examples as much as possible. On a rating scale of one to ten, rate your awareness of the modeled behavior before this exercise, and then rate your awareness of it again as you do the exercise.

1) _____

2) _____

3) _____

4) _____

5) _____

156

Know that there always remains room for improvement, and then constantly improve.

ACTION STEP

Using a three-column diagram, create a list of ten strengths and passions that you possess. In column two, rate that strength or passion from one to ten, knowing there's always room for improvement. In the third column, list those who could benefit from the new and improved you, and explain how.

157

Dare to offer what others don't—it's the straightest line to success.

ACTION STEP

For each type of potential client you find interesting, draw a picture of a "success train." Let the locomotive carry that client (college student, beginning entrepreneur, soon-to-be mother, dad, athlete, etc.). Let each "car" have a listing of each quality the client possesses. Make a second success train with the locomotive named "Gifts, skills, and passions." Let each car demonstrate your various talents and abilities. Now compare the trains and "connect" the corresponding cars. Finally, make a third train with each car representing what competitors do NOT offer these clients that they may appreciate.

1) _____

2) _____

3) _____

4) _____

5) _____

158

> No matter what aspect of your life—professional, personal, mental, physical, relational, or spiritual—remember the importance of having fun along the way.

ACTION STEP

Create a Frayer diagram. Label the four corners "Physical," "Mental," "Spiritual," and "Professional." In each category, list five ways you can incorporate more fun and enjoyment.

1) _____

2) _____

3) _____

4) _____

5) _____

159

Humility is God's gift to help us avoid both arrogance and ignorance.

ACTION STEP

Write a short story incorporating five characters from the same part of US history. Demonstrate in your story how the arrogance or ignorance of these characters serves as the antagonist preventing them from reaching their goals, and how, through self-awareness and personal growth, they overcome those shortcomings.

1) _____

2) _____

3) _____

4) _____

5) _____

160

> *Life is a bunch of todays, so today is the only day that matters.*

ACTION STEP

Create a bucket list. Rather than focusing on things you want to get done before your life ends, focus on the list of items you would want to get done today if today were your last day. What would the most important things be and who would they impact? Can you actually follow through on these things?

1) _____

2) _____

3) _____

4) _____

5) _____

161

> Laughter heals.
> Creating laughter
> is empowering.

ACTION STEP

Create a seven-minute stand-up comedy routine. Perform it during an open mic night and make people laugh. Get video testimonials from a few audience members afterward and ask them what they thought of your comedy and how it made them feel.

1) _____

2) _____

3) _____

4) _____

5) _____

6) _____

7) _____

162

> Directed aggression is the strongest form of action.

ACTION STEP

Research ten people in your community who have successfully channeled their aggression in a positive way to benefit themselves, others, their communities, or their businesses. Create a list of fifteen questions pertaining to this, and interview them for a local newspaper. Legitimately contact the local newspaper and let them know about the interview you've done to see if they would be interested in running it.

1) _____

2) _____

3) _____

4) _____

5) _____

6) _____

7) _____

8) _____

9) _____

10) _____

163

Writing is how we remind ourselves of just how much we know, how strong we are, and how much we have to share with those around us. Writing reminds us how much of a difference we can make in the world.

ACTION STEP

Write as much as you can, whenever and wherever you can. If you aren't in a position to write, such as driving, then make a recording and transcribe it later. Write because everything you have or know has some benefit to someone. Write because revealing the true nature of your humanity demonstrates a strength most don't possess. Write because even in the moments of doubt, frustration, or depression, you are taking action through writing, which serves as the breadcrumbs leading you out.

1) _____

2) _____

3) _____

4) _____

5) _____

164

Persistence, character, creativity, and time are the forgers of greatness.

ACTION STEP

On a Frayer diagram, label the sections "Persistence," "Character," "Creativity," and "Time (patience)." List seven people in each category who embody that quality. Interview them to gain a better understanding of what occurred in their lives to make them embrace that quality.

1) _____

2) _____

3) _____

4) _____

5) _____

165

Balance your time and efforts toward self-improvement with some occasional time spent relaxing; no heavy thoughts or tremendous actions, just committed time to a mindless activity for the purpose of decompression.

ACTION STEP

Compile a list of ten activities that are nothing but fun and, one by one, commit to each of them to give your brain a vacation.

1) _____

2) _____

3) _____

4) _____

5) _____

6) _____

7) _____

8) _____

9) _____

10) _____

By this point, you may be wondering why the book is subtitled, "166 quotable insights to catapult your creativity", when it clearly lists one hundred and sixty five. There be may people who get frustrated. They might feel shortchanged, perhaps even cheated or lied to. There is, in fact, another quote and action step resting within this book. It may not even be noticed if this book is browsed through, certain parts are ignored, or if one has a preconceived notion in advance of where they all will be. Still, the fact remains, that if you go back through the book now having this knowledge to look where you otherwise may not have, you will be surprised at how easy it is to find. You may even notice that it seems to jump off of the page at you.

This final quote and action step were designed with this purpose in mind. The purpose of this book is to help you better understand yourself on a multitude of levels. It is also important to realize that once you DO have a better command of who you are and what you can do, opportunities, much like that final quote, will come to you.

That being said, consider the final quote to be a very simple scavenger hunt teaching the valuable lesson within the quote itself. Be sure, though, that you consider the additional lesson it teaches; how to discover more opportunity within your own life as it pertains to you and those around you.

SELF-EXAMINATION TOOLS

Here is a list of some of the tools available to you. Some include a brief explanation and others have a lengthier explanation.

- "Picture yourself…"

  - *The "Picture yourself…" tool is an excellent strategy for gaining a greater vision of where you want to be rather than where you currently are. In moving the focus of our thoughts from where we are to where we want to be, we allow for a change in attitude as well. This happens through focusing on the desire for something positive rather than the experience of something negative. "Seeing" yourself achieve something makes it much easier to endure whatever is required to attain that goal.*

- Five-question quiz

  - *The five-question quiz enables you to start developing questions in regard to a specific topic. The wonderful feature about this tool is that, with a little practice, the questions start to become sequential in nature. As a result, you start to unlock information within yourself you didn't know existed. From Socrates to private investigators, many of the wisest people understand that the key to gaining information starts with questions, and the secret to obtaining the right kind of information or wisdom rests in asking intelligent, sequential questions.*

- "Describe…"

  - Sometimes having to give a brief description forces us to stop and examine ourselves in a way we may never have before.

- "Draw a diagram of…"

  - Sometimes having a visual just makes good sense.

- Create a pledge/mantra/mission/promise statement

  - The key difference between this and some of the other tools is that these enable a person to set up goals and desires in a specific, achievable format used by many businesses.

- Brainstorm a list

  - The great feature of brainstorming is that it involves more than one person. Others may have a way of viewing you or your life that you don't see. Including them in your brainstorming process opens you up to ideas you may not have arrived at on your own.

- Rating form (rate the following items on a scale of one to ten)

  - Scaling items often allows you to establish different values of things you may never have taken the time to evaluate previously.

- "List the creative qualities of…"

  - Often people tend to get lost in regard to their creative sides, and when asked to "get creative," may draw a blank. The key *is to remember that creativity is applicable to other things. Sometimes in order to jumpstart the creativity, we need to look for creativity within specific thoughts, places, ideas, items, etc. It is the difference between facing a blank canvas and paint versus trying to explain the creative elements of someone else's painting; we need to look toward something else first and then reflect on creativity as it applies within that object or idea.*

- The "me" paragraph

  - In this exercise, you get to write a paragraph telling all about you; the you that you are or the you that you desire to be. Sometimes putting "a little about you" on paper is just what the doctor ordered. Do so consistently for the purpose of reflecting back on it. It allows for a check-up from the neck up.

- Create your life as a fairy tale—be sure they all live happily ever after!

  - Sometimes it helps to add a bit of levity when conducting a self-examination. Fairy tales, though light in nature for the purpose of storytelling to children, also possess many moments of conflict, good vs. evil, and life lessons. More than that, in turning life into a fairy tale, you tap tremendously into creativity.

- Study cards/Index cards

  - *The great feature of study cards or index cards is their handy nature. They enable you to document certain thoughts or notes that serve as constant reminders. Due to the convenient size of the cards, they can be carried anywhere and constantly referred to.*

- **Conduct an interview**

  - *Sometimes the best way to gain perspective is to conduct an interview of someone else. At the least, it offers an opportunity to learn valuable life lessons without having to experience them yourself. At the most, seeing into someone else's life can help us connect with creativity and passion in a way we never realized.*

DIAGRAM SECTION

Attached you will find a list of graphic organizers, diagrams, and formatted charts that can benefit anyone in all walks of life. From diary and journal entries to rating lists and flowcharts, the purpose of these is to satisfy the need to organize thoughts first before applying the action steps for each quote. In providing a form of organized formatting for the thoughts in each task, it becomes much easier to gain clarity in the greater understanding of self. It's like removing the speed bumps from the road; not only does the ride become smoother, it becomes faster and longer as well. In removing the mental speed bumps of the thought process—especially in regard to the critical thought process—we start to develop greater clarity as well as greater purpose. With frustration and distraction removed, the mind is free and clear to run rampant, not only with regard to the tasks presented, but regarding new thoughts beyond the task of the action step. How far can the human mind go? That is a very interesting question. It is a question that this particular author challenges you to explore. After all, the greater the mental journey, the more to be shared with the world.

Concept 1

Concept 2

How alike

How different?

With Regard To

Summarize:

POSITION STATEMENT

REASONS

FACTS

166 QUOTABLE INSIGHTS TO CATAPULT CREATIVITY

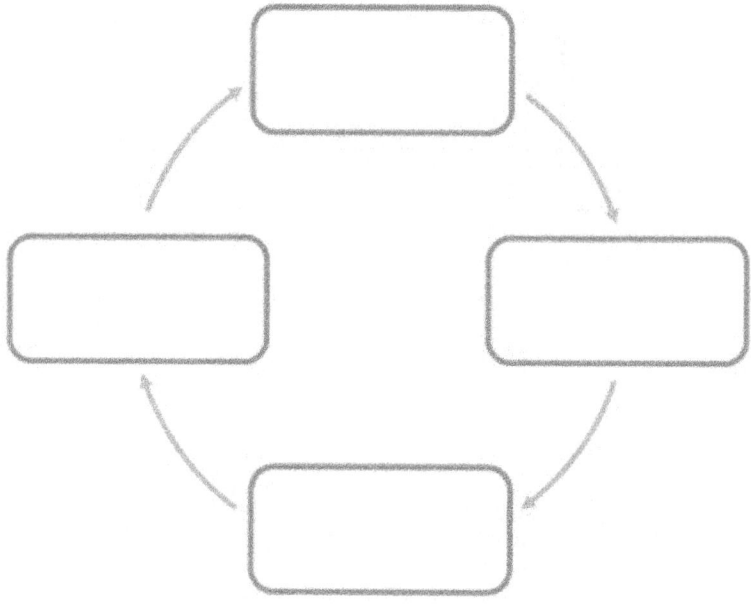

353

Topic

Problem

Solution

Main Idea Sentence

Plus/ Minus/ Intriguing

P(+) Plus	
M(-) Minus	
I(?) Intriguing	

355

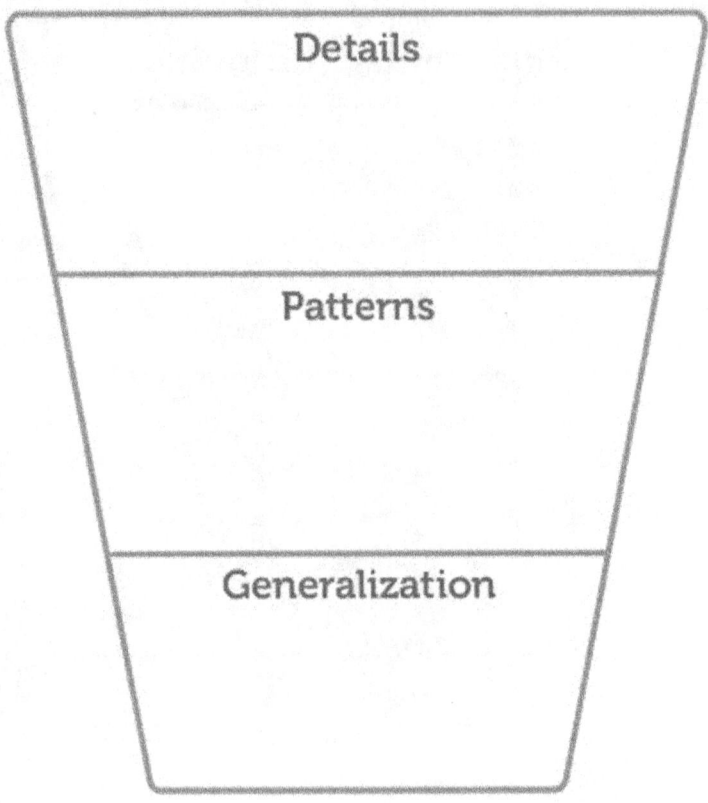

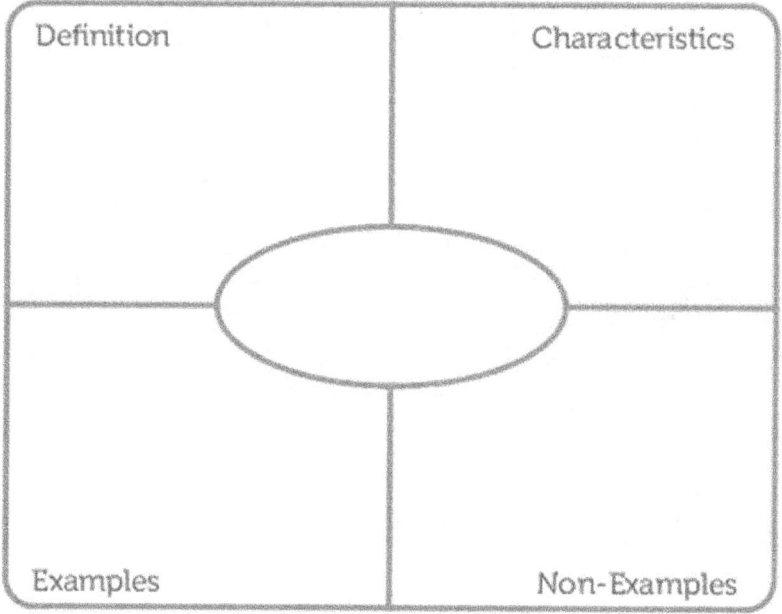

Get Quotivated!

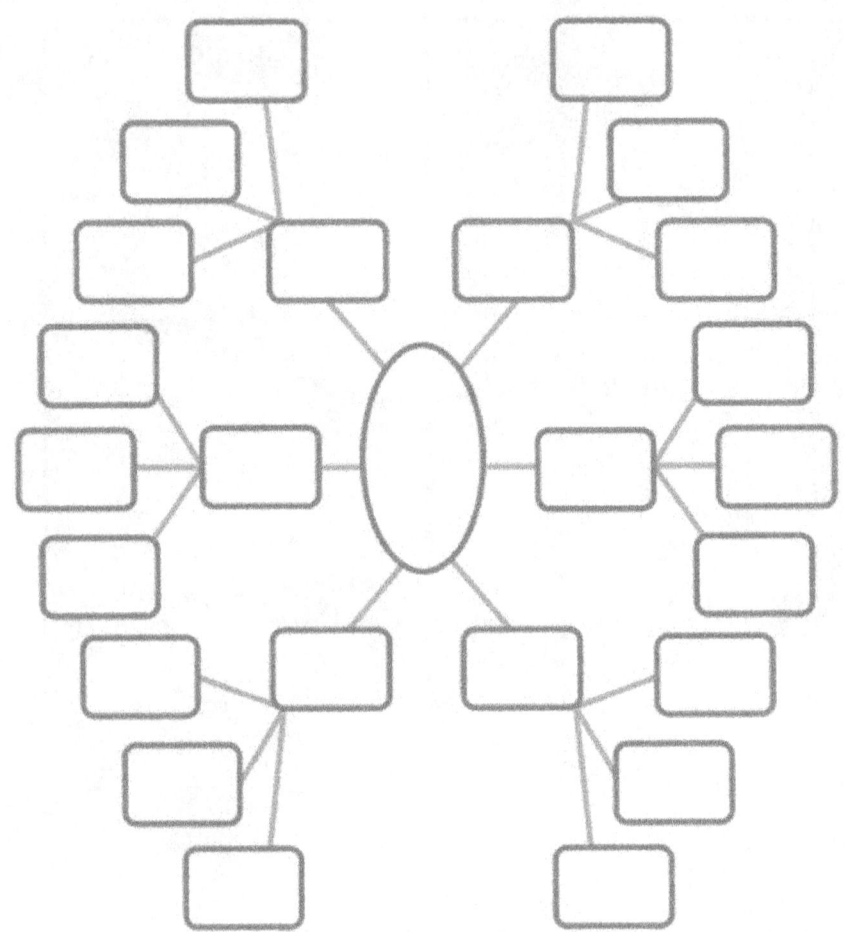

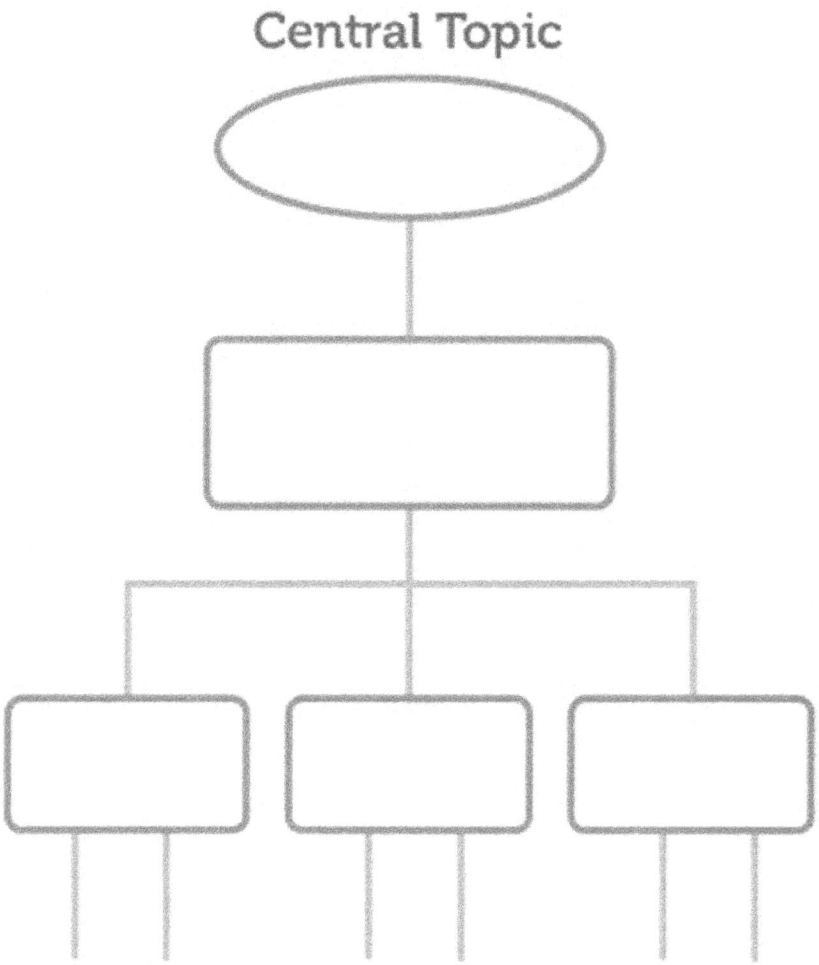

Know	Understand	Do

Cause/Effect
Justification
Error Analysis
Classifying
Evaluation

Compare/Contrast
Induction
Abstracting
Example to Idea
Writing Prompts

Constructing Support
Deduction
Analyzing Perspectives
Idea to Example

Title: _____

Setting: [   ]

Characters: _____ _____
_____ _____
_____ _____
_____ _____

Problem: [   ]

Event 1: _____
Event 2: _____
Event 3: _____
Event 4: _____
Event 5: _____

Solution: [   ]

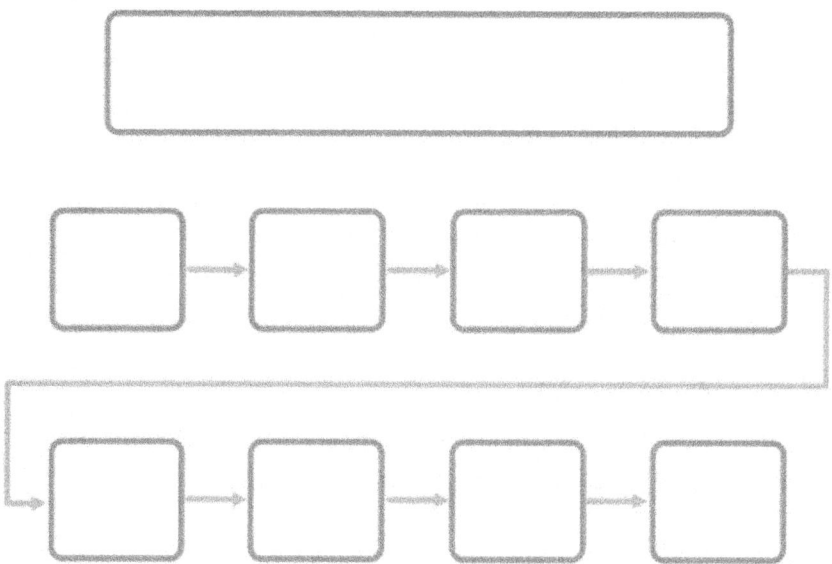

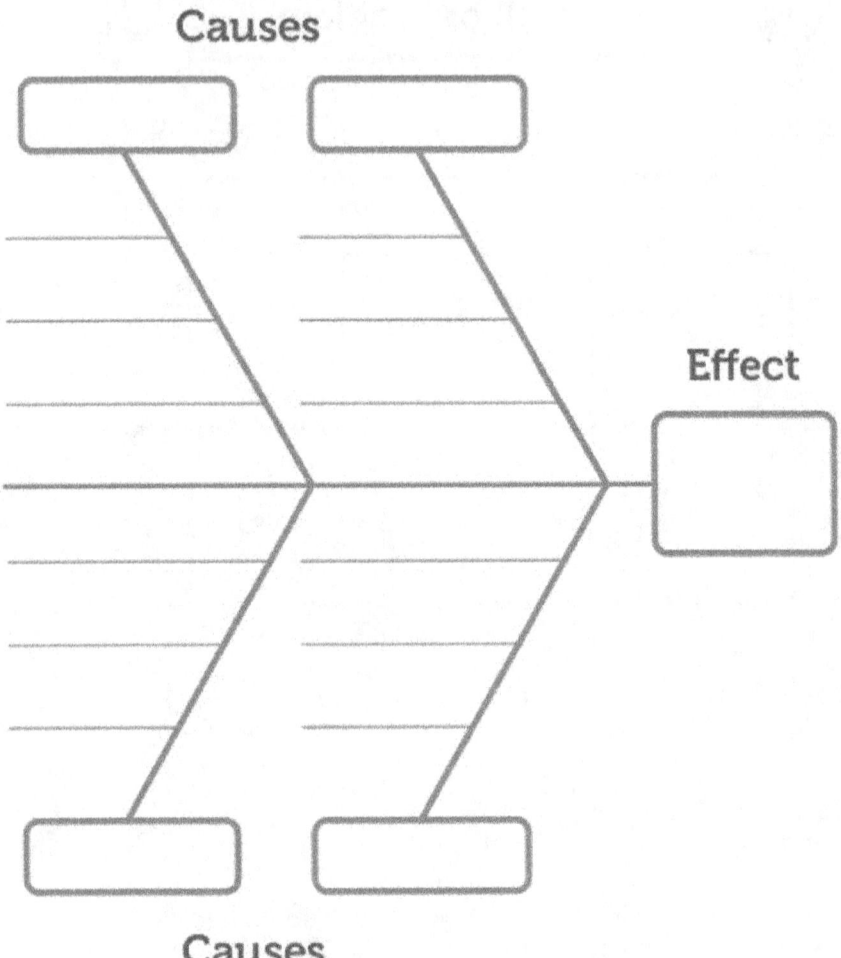

ABOUT THE AUTHOR

Jimmy Leo resides in Tampa Bay Florida with his wife and two daughters. He has been entertaining and connecting with audiences for over twenty years and teaching professionally for eight. With a who's who of clients including The New York Islanders Pro Hockey Organization, Steinway Pianos, & Jetblue Airlines, his knowledge of performance and creativity is second to none.

A former and current record holder, Jimmy has appeared on local and national television. His creativity has enabled him to educate and entertain at schools, colleges, and corporations. Whether his message is catapulting creativity, personal prosperity, or peak presentation skills, Jimmy's innovative approach to creativity CONSTANTLY leaves his audiences in awe.

Jimmy has filmed instructional DVDs on performance & presentation skills. Having written numerous articles on the art, marketing, and psychology of performance and creativity. The demand for his expertise on the topics has resulted in him speaking in New York, Las Vegas, and numerous locations in between. The presenter's presenter, Jimmy Leo is The Creativity Concierge.

For further products and services offered by the Creativity Concierge, contact us at;

727-597-7274

www.creativityconcierge.com

www.ingramcontent.com/pod-product-compliance
Lightning Source LLC
Chambersburg PA
CBHW022101150426
43195CB00008B/216